crazy sexy asian

sexy

/ Sɛksi /

Learn how to pronounce

adjective

1. 1 .

sexually attractive or exciting.

"sexy French underwear"

synonyms:

sexually attractive, seductive , desirable , alluring , inviting ,
sensual , sultry , slinky , provocative , tempting , tantalizing ;
More

nubile , voluptuous , shapely , luscious , lush ;

feline ;

bedroom ;

flirtatious , coquettish ;

informal hot , fanciable , beddable , come-hither , come-to-bed
;

informal fit , mortgage ;

informal foxy , cute , bootylicious;

informal spunky ;

vulgar slang fuck me

"she's so sexy"

erotic , arousing, exciting , stimulating , hot ;

sexually explicit, titillating , suggestive , racy , risqué ,
provocative , spicy , juicy , adult, X-rated ;

ore , coarse , smutty , pornographic , vulgar , crude , lewd ,
lubricious ;

informal raunchy , steamy , naughty , horny , porn , blue , skin ;
informal saucy , fruity ;

informal gamy

"a TV show featuring sexy home videos"

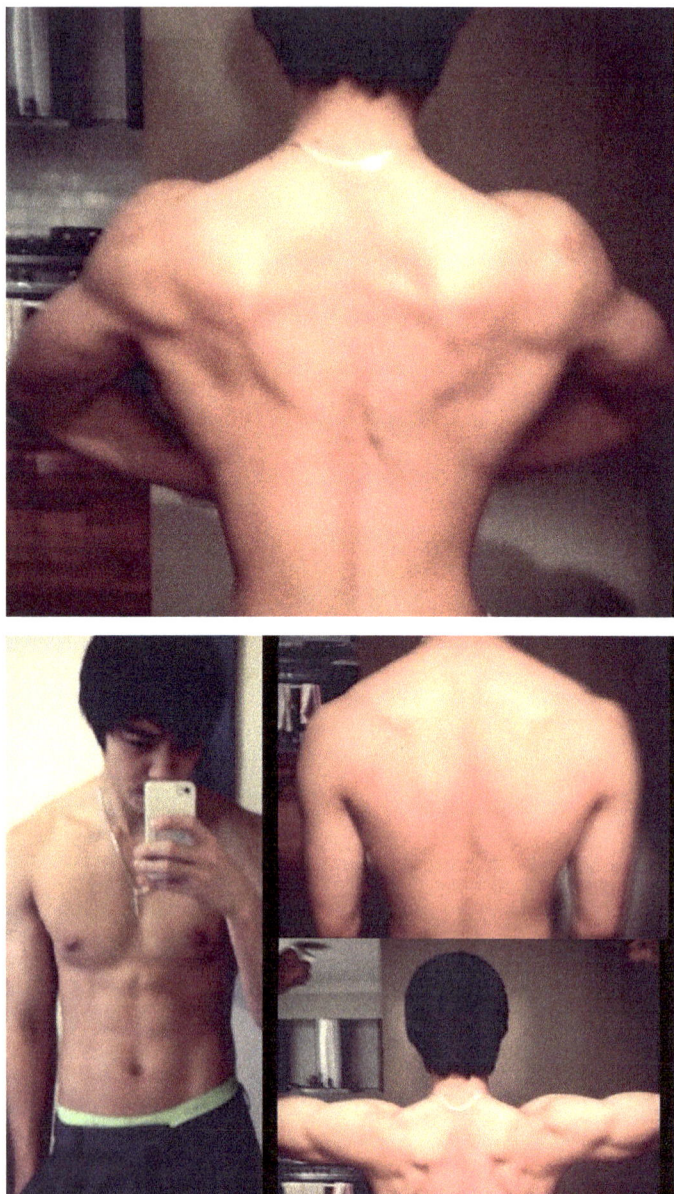

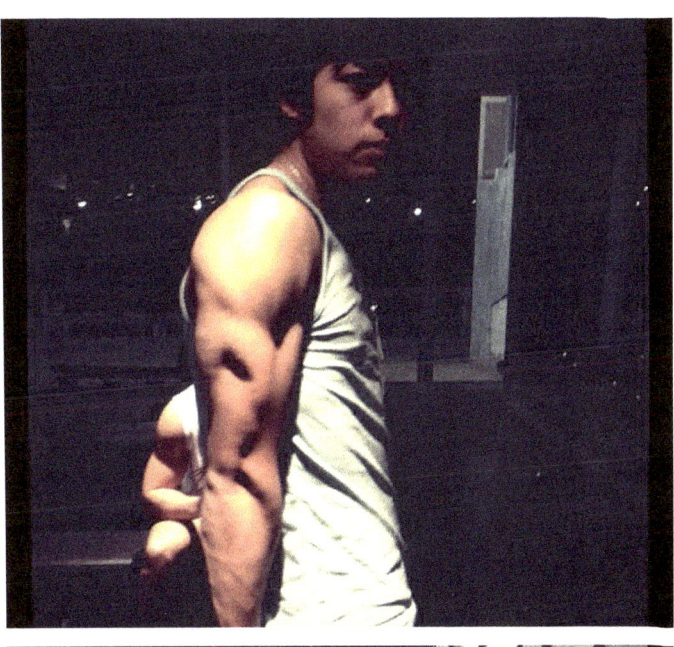
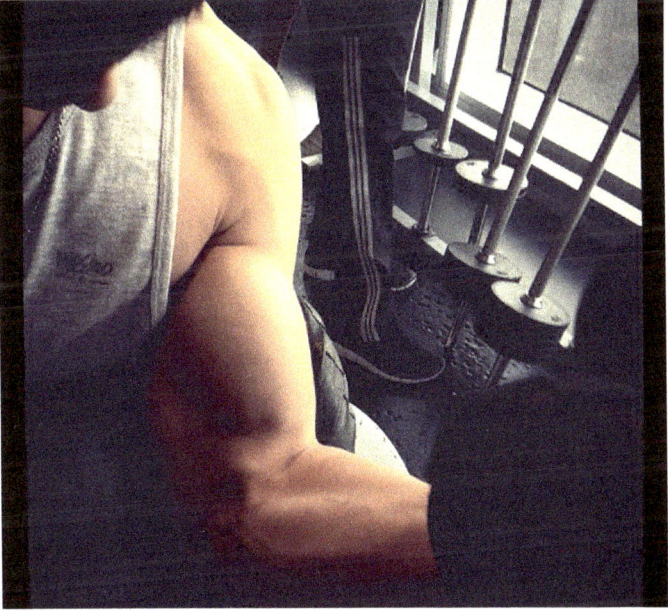

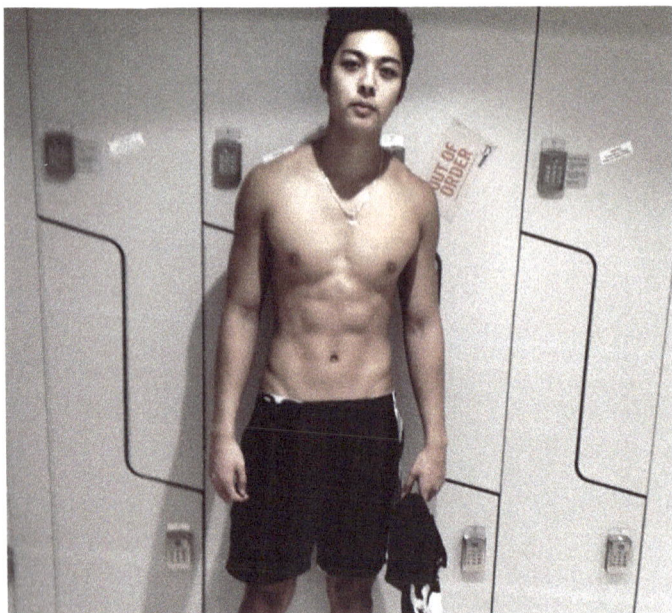

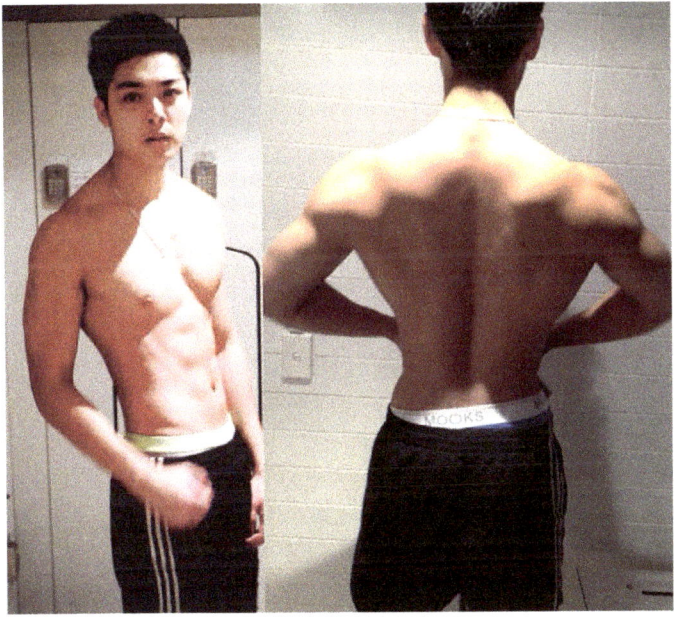

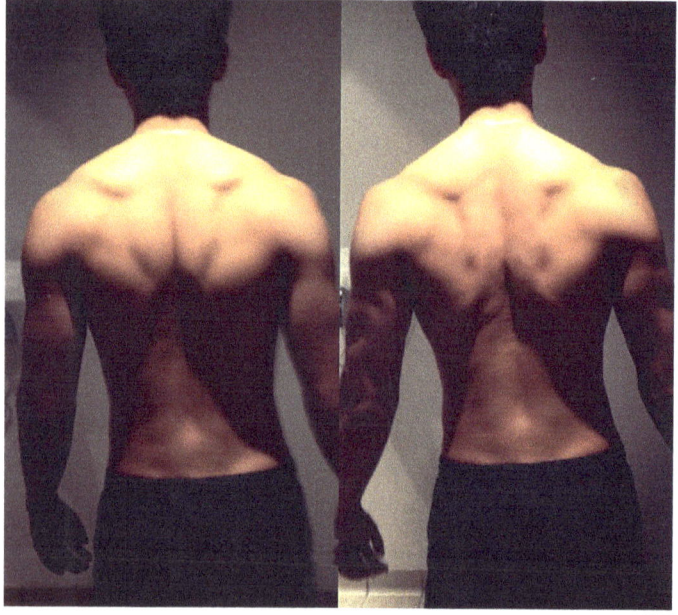

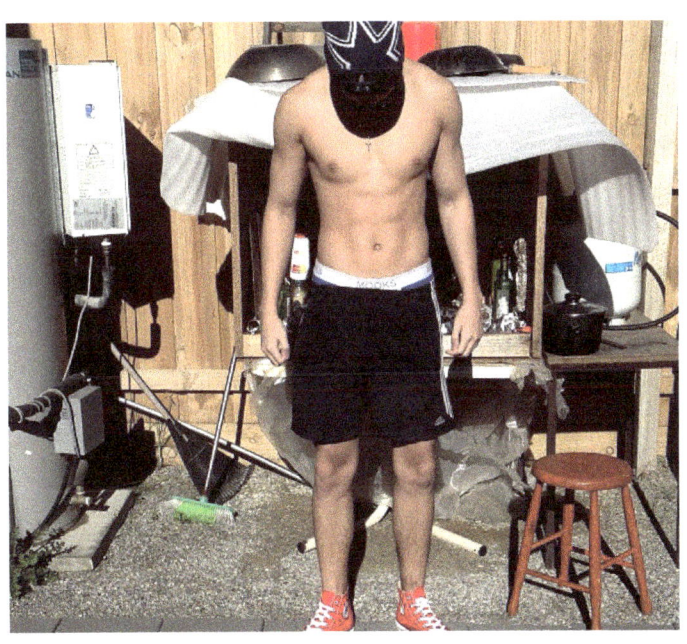

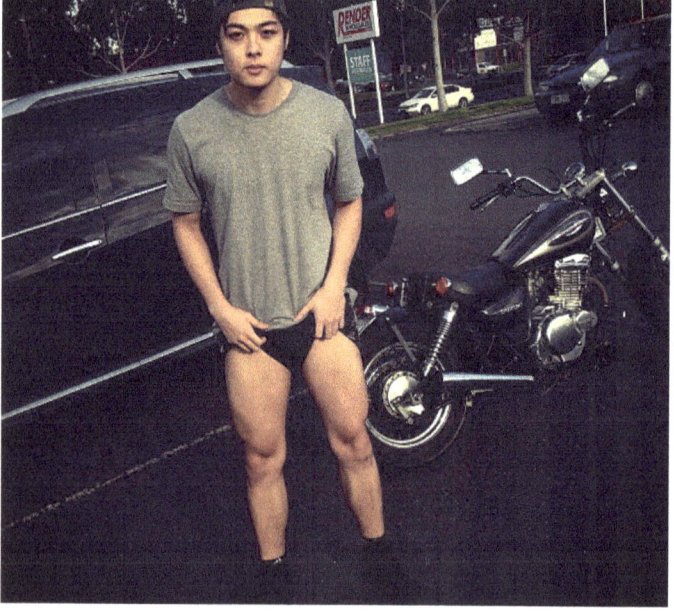

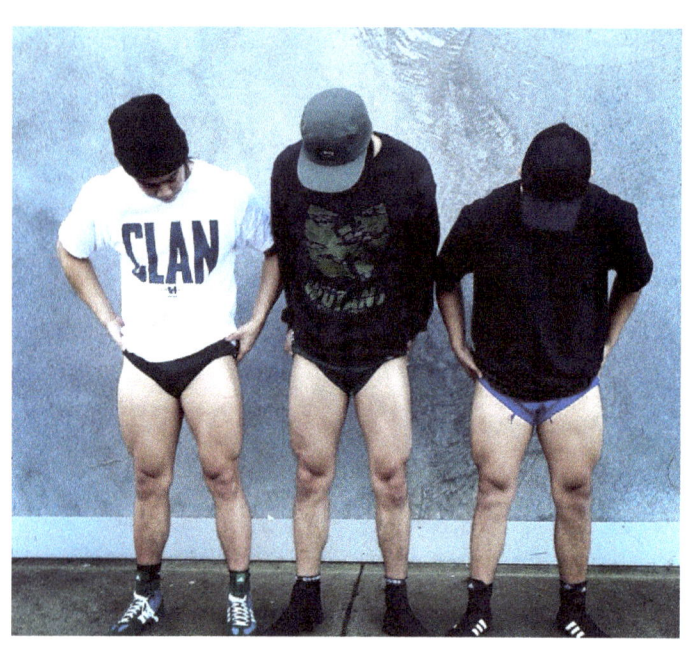

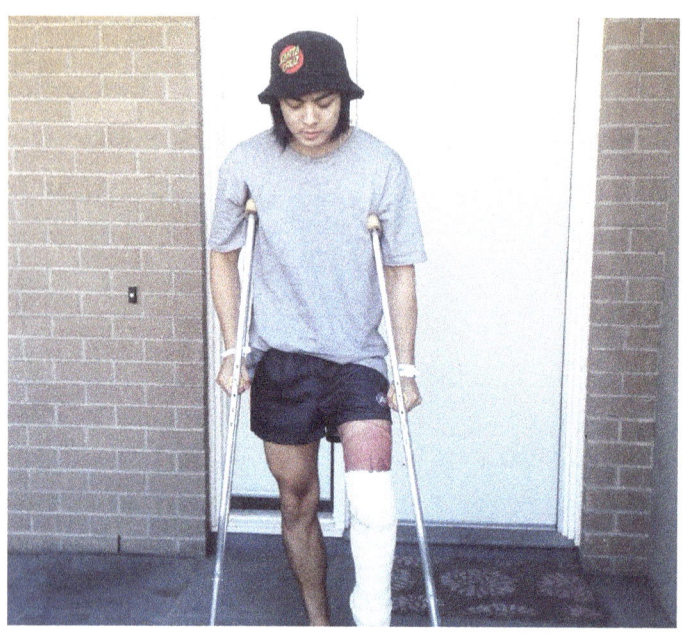

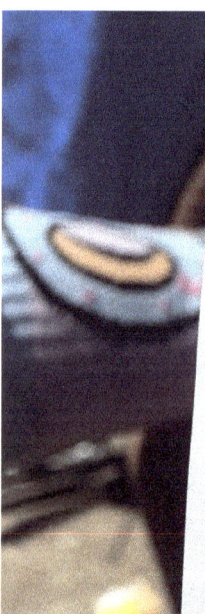

CPSIA information can be obtained
at www.ICGtesting.com
Printed in the USA
BVHW022001280719
554531BV00010B/300/P

9 780464 086369